I0002954

Python

Ultimate Crash Course to Learn It Well and Become an Expert in Python Programming

© **Copyright 2016 by Jamie Logan** **- All rights reserved.**

This document is geared towards providing exact and reliable information in regards to the topic and issue covered. The publication is sold with the idea that the publisher is not required to render accounting, officially permitted, or otherwise, qualified services. If advice is necessary, legal or professional, a practiced individual in the profession should be ordered.

- From a Declaration of Principles which was accepted and approved equally by a Committee of the American Bar Association and a Committee of Publishers and Associations.

In no way is it legal to reproduce, duplicate, or transmit any part of this document in either electronic means or in printed format. Recording of this publication is strictly prohibited and any storage of this document is not allowed unless with written permission from the publisher. All rights reserved.

The information provided herein is stated to be truthful and consistent, in that any liability, in terms of inattention or otherwise, by any usage or abuse of any policies, processes, or directions contained within is the solitary and utter responsibility of the recipient reader. Under no circumstances will any legal responsibility or blame be held against the publisher for any reparation, damages, or monetary loss due to the information herein, either directly or indirectly.

Python

Respective authors own all copyrights not held by the publisher.

The information herein is offered for informational purposes solely, and is universal as so. The presentation of the information is without contract or any type of guarantee assurance.

The trademarks that are used are without any consent, and the publication of the trademark is without permission or backing by the trademark owner. All trademarks and brands within this book are for clarifying purposes only and are the owned by the owners themselves, not affiliated with this document.

Jamie Logan

Table of Contents

Introduction

I want to thank you and congratulate you for downloading the book, *"Python: Ultimate Crash Course to Learn It Well and Become an Expert in Python Programming "*.

This book contains proven steps and strategies on how to learn Python Programming quickly, easily, and thoroughly. It is designed to be a practical and straightforward tutorial of essential Python Programming concepts and techniques that will transform self-learners from beginners to experts in less than two weeks of intensive study. It provides useful and practical examples of the programming concepts presented and makes learning an enjoyable and interesting experience. Python is an easy-to-learn yet powerful and versatile programming language. By devoting a few hours of your time every day, you will acquire the essential skills and confidence to write your own program and automate daily tasks in no time at all.

Thanks again for downloading this book, I hope you enjoy it!

Introduction

Chapter 1: Understanding Python

Python is a high level, object-oriented, interpreted, interactive, and general-purpose programming language.

A high level scripting language, Python programs are intended to be highly readable and easy-to-understand. It uses concise and nearly regular English keywords and implements simple syntax.

Python is an object-oriented programming language which supports user-defined classes, inheritance, and methods binding. In Python, everything can be used as an object. Every object is first class.

Although its object-oriented feature is always emphasized, Python is actually a multi-paradigm programming language which also supports structured, aspect-oriented, and functional programming methods.

Python is an interpreted language. It has to convert programs into machine-readable byte code before it can execute the codes. It is also a compiled language because it has to implicitly perform compilation while loading the modules or implementing standard processes.

Python is an interactive language. You can use the Python prompt to type codes and produce instant feedback from the interpreter.
.

Python is a powerful and versatile language. You can use it to develop office productivity tools that will automate repetitive tasks or simplify complicated jobs. You can also use it to write large web applications, powerful games, and GUIs.

Python's standard library which contains hundreds of useful modules is one of the biggest reasons why it has remained popular across diverse types and generations of users. These libraries or modules are easily accessible through the import keyword and include various internet protocols, network programming, mathematical functions, regular expression matching, random module and functions, email handling, operating systems, GUI toolkit, and XML processing.

Python easily integrates with other languages such as Java, C, C++, ActiveX, and COM. Its support for automatic garbage collection makes it a memory-friendly programming language.

Although it derived many of its syntax and structure from C, Python differs significantly from C in two major aspects: the use of whitespaces or indentation to structure blocks of codes and dynamic typing. While C uses curly braces {} and a semi-colon to mark a group of statements, Python uses indentation to indicate code blocks. In C, a variable is always declared and tied to a specific data type before it can be used. In Python, a variable is not declared and can be reassigned anytime.

Python is a highly readable language that can be learned by anyone to make powerful and useful programs within a short investment of time. It is a beginner-friendly program that is highly recommended for those who are learning to program for the first time.

To use Python, an open source language, you have to download its installation files from the website of Python Software Foundation.

Python

For windows users, you can use this link to find your preferred version:

https://www.python.org/downloads/

For Mac users, you may use this link:

https://www.python.org/downloads/mac-osx/

Chapter 2: Working with IDLE

IDLE, short for Integrated Development Learning Environment, is an IDE created exclusively for use with Python. It is installed alongside the interpreter and documentation files.

IDLE offers a basic graphical user interface with many useful features that make writing programs more intuitive and efficient. It is a flexible and powerful platform for writing, exploring, and running your programs.

You can use IDLE for working in interactive and script mode. In interactive mode, you can use the Python prompt >>> to test each line of code. The interpreter evaluates every statement entered while simultaneously executing statements in active memory. In script mode, also called the normal mode, the interpreter runs scripts or files saved with a .py extension.

The most important features of IDLE include the Python Shell, multiple-window, integrated text editor, smart indent, syntax highlighting, auto-completion, and an integrated debugger.

The Python Shell

The Python Shell offers a user-friendly and efficient interface, a simple drop down menu, and several editing features. You can use it to work interactively with Python. You can scroll back, copy paste, edit, and review previously-entered statements. You will need it to access the text editor window which you can use to write and run your programs or modules.

You can try it out by entering some expressions. For example, you can use the print() function to display the string 'I love Python!' onscreen:

At the >>> prompt, simply type and enter:

>>>print("I love Python!")

On the succeeding line, the interpreter will output:

I love Python!

You can also type and enter the same string without using the print() function. Python will simply return the string.

>>> "I love Python!"
'I love Python!'

You may use the Python Shell as a calculator for solving basic mathematical expressions. Just type and enter the expression and Python should be able to solve it in seconds.

Examples:

>>> 4 * 6
24

>>> 18 / 3
6

>>> 6 + 4
10

>>> 27 − 4
23

The Text Editor

You can access the text editor through the file option of the Python Shell. Clicking on 'New File' opens an integrated text editor which you can use to type, edit, save, and run your programs. You can also use it to open another text editor window. It offers basic options for editing, formatting, and running modules.

The format menu provides several useful options for indenting/dedenting, toggling/untoggling comments, paragraph formatting, removing trailing whitespaces, and setting tabs or indent width.

The run menu allows you to check and run your module. The output is displayed on the Python Shell.

<u>Writing Your First Python Program</u>

You can use any other type of text editor but to familiarize yourself with Python's integrated environment, you will use IDLE's built-in text editor for your first program and the succeeding programs in this book.

Accessing the Text Editor

To open a new text editor window on Python Shell:

Click on File
Choose New File

Typing your program

Once it opens, you can start typing your first program on the text editor.

You first program will be the universal program: "Hello, World!"

Type the following line on the text editor:

print(Hello, World!)

Saving the File

Saving the file prepares it for processing by Python and allows you to work on your program on a partial basis. You can save the program on a specific directory on your hard disk or in any storage device.

To save the file:

Click on File
Choose Save

The Save option opens a 'Save as' dialogue box which will allow you to save your file on a preferred destination folder other than the default folder. Files you save automatically gets the .py extension. For example, if you save this file as 'HelloProgram', Python will automatically append the .py extension and save it as HelloProgram.py.

Running the Program

For your program to be successful, the interpreter must be able to run it without error or exceptions.

To run the program, you have to click on the Run menu. This will open three options: Python Shell, Check Module, and Run Module.

Choose Run Module to run your program. If no errors are found, the Python shell will display:

```
======= RESTART: C: /Python/HelloProgram.py
=======
Hello, World!
```

Exiting Python

To exit from the Python Shell, you can type exit() or quit() and press enter. You may also type ctrl-d.

To exit the command line, you can type exit() or quit() and press enter.

Working with Files and Directories

There is always a current working directory and this is where Python will save your file or access the files you want to open or import. Python manages files and directories through its os module which contains useful methods for creating, changing, or removing directories.

The mkdir() Method

You can use the mkdir method to create a new directory in the default directory. It only requires one argument: the name of the directory that you want to create.

syntax:
os.mkdir("newdir")

For instance, if you want to create a directory named 'newprograms', you can use the code:

```
import os

# Create a directory "newprograms"
os.mkdir("newprograms")
```

The chdir() Method

The chdir() method is useful when you have to work on a file which is stored in another directory. It has one argument: the name of the directory that you want to use.

syntax:

os.chdir("newdir")

For example, if you are presently working on a file located in the directory Programs/Python/games and you want to change to the Programs/Python/sciapps, you can use the following codes:

```
import os

# Change a directory to "Programs/Python/sciapps"
os.chdir("Programs/Python/sciapps")
```

The getcwd() Method

The current working directory is the directory that Python stores in memory. Whenever you enter commands like 'import file.txt', Python will locate the file in the current working directory. To display the current working directory, you can use the getcwd() method.

Syntax:
os.getcwd()

Example:

import os

This gives the location of current working directory

os.getcwd()

The rmdir() Method

The rmdir() method is used to delete a directory. It has one argument, the name of the directory to be deleted. Take note that you have to delete all contents of the directory before you can delete it. In addition, you have to provide the full name of the directory.

syntax:

os.rmdir('dirname')

Here's an example:

import os

# Remove "/pyprog/sciapp" directory.
os.rmdir("/pyprog/sciapp")

Chapter 3: Basic Syntax

Syntax refers to the set of rules that define the correct form and sequence of words and symbols in a programming language. This chapter will discuss the syntax and conventions used in Python3.

Python Keywords

Python has 33 keywords that are reserved for built-in functions and processes. You have to be aware of these keywords and avoid using them as identifier in your programs.

True	False	None
while	for	return
continue	break	pass
if	elif	else
class	def	del
import	from	lambda
and	or	not
finally	nonlocal	global
with	raise	as
assert	except	yield
try	is	in

Naming Conventions for Identifiers

An identifier is a name given to a variable, string, dictionary, list, class, module, function, and all other objects in Python. Each type of object has its own naming convention.

11

In general, an identifier may consist of one letter or a combination of uppercase and lowercase letters, underscores, or the digits 0 to 9.

Examples of Identifier:

X
x
my_dict
my_list9
UPPERCASE
lowercase
UPPERCASE_WITH_UNDERSCORES
lowercase_with_underscores
CamelCase or CapWords
mixedCase

You should not use keywords are identifier but if you really need to use one, you can distinguish it from a keyword by using a trailing underscore. This is preferred over abbreviation or word corruption.

For example: global_, class_

Identifiers should not contain symbols or special characters such as #, $, %, and @.

Identifiers may end in a number but should never start with a number. For example, var_1 is valid but 1var is not.

A multiple-word identifier is acceptable but separating each unit with an underscore will make it more readable.

For example, my_main_function is more preferred over mymainfunction.

You can use the following style guide when naming specific identifiers:

Global Variables

Names of global variables are written in lower case. If there are two or more words in an identifier, they are preferably separated by an underscore for clarity and readability.

Classes

The UpperCaseCamelCase convention is used when naming a class. That is, the identifier should start with an uppercase letter. If there are two or more words in a class identifier, they all start in a capital letter and are joined together. For example:

Employees, MyCamelCase, TheFamousList, Cars, MyCar

Instance Variables

Names of instance variables consisting of two or more words should be separated by underscore(s). They should be written in lowercase.

Examples: student_one, member_status, employee,

Functions

A function name should be written in lowercase. Multiple-word function names should be separated by an underscore for better readability.

Examples: multiplier, adder, sub_function

Arguments

Arguments must consist of letters in lowercase. The word 'self' is always the first argument in instance methods while 'cls' is the first argument in class methods.

Modules and Packages

Module identifiers should be in lowercase and are usually written as short single-word name. Using multiple words is discouraged but you may do so to facilitate clarity and readability. A single underscore should separate each unit in module and package identifier consisting of two or more words.

Constants

Constants are written in uppercase letters and separated by an underscore if the name consists of multiple words.

Examples: TOTAL, MAX_OVERFLOW

Quotation Marks

Quotation marks are used to indicate strings. You may use single ('), double ("), or triple (''') quotes but you must use the same mark to start and end string literals.

Examples:

'status', "Johnny", '''age limit: ''', 'Enter a vowel: '

Indentation

Python uses indentation or white spaces to structure programs or blocks of codes. You will not use curly braces {} to distinguish a group of related statements. Instead, you will use equal indentation to mark a block of code. For this reason, Python programs look neat, clutter-free, organized, and readable. A nested block is created by indenting a block further to the right.

While you can use tabs to indent a code, Python programmers commonly use four white spaces to mark a block of code. This is a language convention that you should consider for uniformity. It is not strictly imposed, however and you may use tabs instead. Just don't forget to make sure that all lines in a code block are indented consistently if you want your program to run as expected. When using the built-in text editor, you will notice that it intuitively provides four white spaces whenever it is expected based on the most recently typed statement.

Here is a snippet of a program that will give you an idea of how Python programs are structured:

```
def Vehicle_Rental(days):
    rate = 15 * days
    if days >= 15:
        rate -= 20
    elif days >= 7:
        rate -= 5
    return fees
```

Statements

Statements are expressions that may be entered on the Python prompt or written inside a program and are read and executed by the interpreter. Python supports statements such as 'if, 'for', 'while', 'break', and assignment statements.

Multiple-line statements

Some statements may span over one line of code and stretch to several lines. An implicit way to tell Python that the lines are related and form a single statement is by enclosing the statements in parentheses (), curly braces {}, or square brackets [].

For example, the following assignment statement creates a list and will require 3 lines of codes. The items are enclosed in square brackets which indicate that they belong to a list and are part of a single statement.

```
>>>   my_collection  =  ['stamps',  'stationery',  'pens',
       'compact discs', 'boxes',
                   'watches',    'metallic    toy    cars',
       'numismatic coins',
                   'paintings',  'newspaper    clippings',
'books']
```

You may also indicate continuation explicitly by using a backslash \ at the end of each line of related statements. For example:

```
my_alphabet = 'a', 'b', 'c', 'd','e', 'f', 'g', 'h', 'i' \
           'j', 'k', 'l' 'm', 'n', 'o', 'p', 'q', 'r' \
           's', 't', 'u','v', 'w', 'x', 'y', 'z'
```

Documentation String

A docstring, short for documentation string, is used to provide information on what a class or a function does.

Docstrings are typically found at the top of a code block that defines a class, function, method, or module. By convention, a docstring starts with a one-line imperative phrase that begins in a capital letter and ends with a period. It may stretch over multiple lines and are enclosed in triple double quotes (""").

Here are examples of a docstring:

```
def adder(x, y):
    """Function to get the sum of two numbers."""
    return x + y


class Doc(obj):

    """ Explain function docstring.
```

A function name is introduced by the keyword def. Function definition statements end in a colon and are followed immediately by a docstring in triple double quotes. The function body is distinguished by the white spaces right after the definition statement and docstring.
```
    """
```

Comments

Comments are notes written inside programs. They are intended to provide documentation about the programming steps, processes, and other information that a programmer may consider important. Comments are useful when evaluating a program. They facilitate a smooth review and transition between programmers. A hash # symbol is used to introduce a comment. It tells Python to ignore the line and proceed to the execution of the next statement.

For example:

```
#print a birthday greeting
print('Happy Birthday, Member!')
```

Comments may stretch over multiple lines. You may use a hash # symbol at the start of each line to wrap the lines together.

Example:

```
#This step is important
# because it is the basis
# of succeeding processes.
```

Another way to wrap long multiple-line comment is by using triple quotes at the beginning and end of the comment.

For example:

```
"""This is another way
to write comments that
span several lines."""
```

Chapter 4: Variables and Python Data Types

Variables

A variable points to a reserved location in a computer's memory. Variables can be used to store, save, access, or retrieve data from the assigned memory location. Creating a variable means allocating space in memory. Variables are given specific names to identify the memory location associated with them. These names are used to instruct your computer to save, access, edit, or retrieve data.

Creating and managing variables in Python is both straightforward and flexible. To create a variable, you can use an appropriate name and assign a value with the assignment operator (=). Python intuitively identifies the data tape based on the values assigned to variables. You need not declare that a variable contains a particular data type.

These are examples of variable assignment statements:

```
x = "fruits"          # a string
average = 90.50       # a floating point number
num = 25              # an integer
note = "incomplete"       # a string
```

In a variable assignment statement, the left operands refer to the names of the variables while the right operand states the value assigned to the variable.

You can check the memory location of the variables defined above by using the id() operator.

```
>>> id(x)
```

54254304

>>> id(average)
51227904

>>> id(num)
1489254544

>>> id(note)
51395944

Python accepts several assignments in a single statement
with the syntax:

a, b, c = 1, 2, 3

Multiple variable assignments follow the positional order.
In the above example:

a = 1, b = 2, and c = 3.

Likewise, Python accepts the assignment of a common
value to multiple variables in a single statement using the
syntax:

a = b = c = "letters"

The above statement assigns "letters", a string, to variables
a, b, and c simultaneously.

Again, you can check if the variables a, b, and c refer to the
same memory location by using the id() operator.

>>> id(a)

51452256

>>> id(b)
51452256

>>> id(c)
51452256

You can easily change the data type and value stored in a variable by reassigning it.

To illustrate, you can create a variable named 'number' and assign an integer value of 30.

number = 30

To increase the value stored in the variable by 20, enter this statement on the Python prompt:

>>>number + = 20

To see how Python evaluates the above expressions, you can use the print function to view the value contained in the variable.

>>>print(number)

You should see this value on the succeeding line:

50

The above example illustrates how easily you can replace the value of a variable with just one statement. The following example will now prove that you can reassign a value with a different data type to the same variable. Assuming you want to replace the value stored in the variable number with the string "trading floor", you can just type the regular assignment statement:

```
>>>number = "trading floor"
```

To check how the assignment statement affected the value stored in the variable number, you can invoke the print function:

```
>>>print(number)
```

The output would be:

trading floor

Data Types

Programming involve simple to complex data processing work. The use of data types allows programmers to organize and work on different data categories. Python supports the following built-in data types:

Number
String
List
Tuple
Set
Dictionary
Booleans
Bytes and byte arrays

Since everything is an object in Python, you will find other data types such as function, method, class, and module.

Numbers

Python 3 supports 3 numeric data types, namely, integers, floating point numbers, and complex numbers. Python will not require you to declare the specific type of a number. It can tell an integer from a float because a floating point number uses a decimal point while an integer does not. It recognizes a complex number because of its standard a + bJ format.

Integers (int)

Integers are whole numbers without a decimal point or fractional part. This number type includes zero, positive, or negative whole numbers and can have unlimited size. Python supports normal integers, octal, hexadecimal, and binary literals.

Normal integers

Examples: 32, 0, -65, 987654321123456789

Octal literal (base 8)

An octal literal is a number with a 0O (zero and uppercase 'O') or 0o (zero and lowercase 'o') prefix.

Examples:

```
>>> 0O34
28

>>> octal_lit = 0O34
>>> print(octal_lit)
28
```

Hexadecimal literal (base 16)

A hexadecimal literal is indicated by an 0X (zero and uppercase 'X') or 0x (zero and lowercase 'x') prefix.

Examples:

>>> 0XA0F
2575

>>> hex_lit = 0xA0F
>>>print(hex_lit)
2575

Binary literal (base 2)

Binary literals are identified y the 0B (zero and uppercase 'B') or 0b (zero and lowercase 'b').

Examples:

>>> 0b101010
42

>>> bin_lit = 0b101010
>>> print(bin_lit)
42

How to Convert Integers to String

The function oct(), hex(), and bin() are used to convert an integer to its string equivalent.

For example, convert the integer 35 to octal, hexadecimal, and binary literals:

integer to octal literal

```
>>> oct(35)
'0o43'
```

integer to hexadecimal literal

```
>>> hex(35)
'0x23'
```

integer to binary literal:

```
>>> bin(35)
'0b100011'
```

Floating-Point Numbers (Floats)

Floating point numbers are real numbers with a decimal point and fractional part.

Examples:

9.55, 210354.95, 12.89, 0.65

Floats can also be expressed in scientific notation where the letter 'e' is used to indicate the 10th power.

```
>>> 9.3e4
93000.0
```

```
>>> 12.2e3
12200.0
```

Complex Numbers

A complex number is a pair of a real and imaginary numbers. Its format is 'a + bJ' or 'a + bj' where the left number is a real number while the right number is a combination of a float (b) and an imaginary number (J). The letter 'J' or 'j' refers to the square root of -1 which is an imaginary number.

For example:

```
>>> a = 3 + 4j
>>> b = 1 - 2j
>>> ab = a + b
>>> print(ab)
(4+2j)
```

Converting From One Numeric Type to Another

Python can handle the conversion of mixed number types to a common type. Sometimes, however, you may have to convert explicitly from one number type to another to comply with syntax requirements. You can compel Python to do the conversion by using the right keyword and parameter.

Converting an integer to a floating-point number:

Type float(x)

```
>>> float(250)
250.0
```

Converting a float to a normal integer:

Type int(x)

```
>>> int(130.5)
130
```

Converting an integer to a complex number:

Type complex(x)

```
>>> complex(62)
(62+0j)
```

Converting a float to a complex number:

Type complex(x)

```
>>> complex(25.6)
(25.6+0j)
```

Converting a numeric pair expression to a complex number:

Type complex(x, y)

```
>>> complex (2, 5)
(2+5j)
```

Strings

A string is an ordered series of Unicode characters consisting of a combination of one or several letters, numbers, or special symbols. It is an immutable data type which means that you can no longer modify the string once it is created.

To create a string, you must place it inside single (') or double quotes (") and assign it to a variable.

```
>>> single_string_ = 'string in single quotes'
>>> double_string = "string in double quotes"
```

If you need to use a single quote or an apostrophe within a string enclosed in a single quote, you have to escape both by placing a backslash (\) before the single quote or apostrophe.

For instance, to create a string 'This is my friend's laptop.' :

```
>>> a_string = 'This is my friend\'s laptop.'
```

You can use the print function to print a_string.

```
>>> print(a_string)
This is my friend's laptop.
```

In like manner, you should escape a double quote inside a string enclosed within double quotes by using the backslash (\).

Hence, when creating the string "She said: "Welcome to the Forum! "", you will use the backslash before the double quotes:

```
>>> double_string = She said:\ "Welcome to the
Forum!\""
```

```
>>> print(double_string)
She said:"Welcome to the Forum!"
```

If you have to use a backslash inside a string, you need to escape the backlash with another backslash.

Hence, to create a string with a backlash symbol "You need a backlash to escape another backlash \":

```
>>> escape_string = "You need a backlash to escape
another backlash \\."
>>> print(escape_string)
You need a backlash to escape another backlash \.
```

Accessing Characters in a String

You can access each character in a string by indexing and a range of characters by slicing.

String Indexing

The first character in a string has zero as its index number while the succeeding characters take 1, 2, 3, 4, and so on. You can also access the string backwards where the last character takes negative 1 as index. To illustrate string indexing, define a variable a_string and assign the string "Programming World".

To access the first character on a_string, you can enter the variable name "a_string" and enclose zero (0) inside the square brackets or index operator [].

```
>>> a_string[0]
'P'
```

To access the character on index 7, just enclose 7 inside the square brackets:

```
>>> a_string[7]
'm'
```

To access the character on index 6:

```
>>> a_string[6]
' m'
```

To access the last character of the string, you can use negative indexing to return the value:

```
>>>a_string[-1]
'g'
```

Since a string is an ordered list, the penultimate letter takes -2 index and so on.

Hence, -5 index is:

```
>>> a_string[-5]
'W'
```

A more technical way to go about accessing the last character is with the use of the len() function. This will be more useful when creating a program. First, you'll use the len() function to determine the size of a string, meaning, the number of characters in a string.

For example, to get the size of the variable 'a_string', you will use the syntax:

```
>>> len(a_string)
18
```

As you have learned earlier, the first character has zero index. Hence, the last character has an index which is one less than the length of the string. To access the last character, you can subtract 1 from the result of the len() function.

For example, type this statement on the Python prompt:

```
>>> a_string[len(a_string)-1]
'g'
```

Slicing Strings

The range [:] slice operator is used to access a range of characters in a string and to create substrings. The first index refers to the first character of the substring while the second index indicates the first character to be excluded in the substring.

There are two ways to go about it. The first is to directly slice the string with the syntax:

```
>>> "Slicers"[2:5]
'ice'
```

```
>>> "Programming"[4:10]
'rammin'
```

Another way, which is what you would normally use in a program, is by assigning the string to a variable then performing the slicing operation on the variable.

For Example:

```
>>> var_1 = "Slicing Strings"
>>> var_1[4:11]
'ing Str'
```

```
>>> var_1[3:13]
'cing Strin'
```

You can drop the first index if the starting character of the substring is also the initial character of the original string.

```
>>> var_1[:7]
'Slicing'
```

Similarly, you can drop the last index if the substring also ends on the last character of the string. For example:

```
>>> var_1[8:]
'Strings'
```

Concatenating Strings

A number of strings can be combined to form one string with the use of the + operator. For instance, to concatenate the strings "I", "am", "a", "Python", "Programming", "Student", you can type and enter the following:

```
I" + "am" + "a" + "Python" + "Programming" + "Student"
```

The output would be:

```
'IamaPythonProgrammingStudent'
```

You can also concatenate strings which are stored in two or more variables. For instance:

```
string_1 = "movie"
string_2 = "is"
string_3 = "worth watching"
print("A great " + string_1 + " " + string_2 + " " + string_3 +".")
```

When you run the code, the output would be:

A great movie is worth watching.

All the indexing, slicing, and concatenation you've done to the string in the preceding examples do not, in any way, affect the string stored in the variable. That's because a string is immutable. This does not mean, however, that you cannot delete or replace a string once it is assigned to a variable. Because variables are flexible, you can always reassign it to a new string which will replace the old string stored in it.

Repeating a String

If you want to repeat a string or a concatenation of strings, you can use the operator * and an integer to indicate how many times you want the string to be repeated.

For example, to repeat the string ^('-')^ three times, you can type it on the Python prompt and specify the number of repetition with *3.

```
>>> "^('-')^" *3
```

Here's what the statement returns:

```
'^('-')^^('-')^^('-')^'
```

Likewise, you can store the string in a variable and apply the * operator on the variable to achieve similar result:

```
>>> symbol_string = "^('-')^"
>>> symbol_string * 3
'^('-')^^('-')^^('-')^'
```

Using the upper() and lower() functions

The upper() and lower() functions are used to display the entire string in uppercase or lowercase respectively.

For example, you can define a variable 'cap_var' that will store the string "capitalization".

>>>cap_var = "Capitalization"

To display the string in uppercase, just type:
>>>print(cap_var.upper())

You should get this output:

CAPITALIZATION

This time, to print the entire string in lowercase, you can type:

print(cap_var.lower())

You'll get the output:

capitalization

As stated, all these operations on the string will not change the actual string stored in cap_var. To prove this, enter the statement:

>>>print(smart_var)
Capitalization

Using the str() function

The str() function allows non-string characters to be converted to string characters. This function is particularly useful when you need to print non-string characters such as integers as string characters.

To illustrate, create a variable that will store the integer 152. This variable may be used later as a parameter for the str() function.

```
>>> my_num = 152
>>> str(my_number)
'152'
```

Hence, to print the string "My student number is 152." you can type this:

```
>>> print("My student number is " + str(my_num))
My student number is 152.
```

Converting an integer to a sting with the use of the str() function does not change the data type of the value stored in my_num. You can prove it by using the type() function on my_num:

```
>>> type(my_num)
<class 'int'>
```

List

List is one of the most commonly used sequence type in Python. A list can contain any type of items such as string, integer, float, etc. It can hold any number of items and a combination of several data types. A list can also contain a list as an element.

To create a list, you can define a variable to contain an ordered series of items separated by a comma. A square bracket is used to enclose the items.

To create an empty list, the syntax is:

my_list = []

To create a list of items, the syntax is:

a_list = [item1, item2, item3, item4]

Here are examples of list creation statements:

color_list = ["yellow", "blue", red", green", "orange"] #list of strings
num_list = [0, 3, 6, 9, 12, 15]
    #list of integers
mixed_list = [10, "mouse", 5.10]   #list of mixed data types
nested_list = ["monitor", 10.2, 4, [6, 5, 1, 2, 4.2, 3]]
    #list with nested list

Accessing Elements on a List

There are different ways to access items on a list:

Indexing

You can use the index operator [] to access the elements of a list. Just like strings, the first item has zero index. When accessing items through its index, you must make sure that you're using an integer in order to avoid getting TypeError. Accessing an element which is beyond the index range will prompt an IndexError.

For example, here is a list of dog breeds:

```
>>> dog_list = ["Chihuahua", "Rottweiler", "Pug",
"Beagle", "Shih Tzu", "Pomeranian"]
```

To access the elements of the dog_list, place the index inside the square brackets:

```
>>> dog_list[0]
'Chihuahua'
```

```
>>> dog_list[3]
'Beagle'
```

```
>>> dog_list[4]
'Shih Tzu'
```

Any attempt to access a non-existent index will result to an IndexError:

```
>>> dog_list[6]
Traceback (most recent call last):
  File "<pyshell#12>", line 1, in <module>
    dog_list[6]
IndexError: list index out of range
```

It is also possible to access a nested list by using nested indexing.

Here's a nested list:

```
>>> nested_list = [6, "subject", 13.5, [2, 5, 8, 11, 14]]
```

To access different elements of the nested list:

```
>>> nested_list[0]
6
```

```
>>> nested_list[1][4]
'e'

>>> nested_list[1][6]
't'

>>> nested_list[3]
[2, 5, 8, 11, 14]

>>> nested_list[3][4]
14
```

Using Negative Indexing to Access List Items

Python also allows negative indexing for lists. The last item has the -1 index, the penultimate item the -2 index, and so on.

For example:

```
>>>string_list = ["m", "u", "t", "a", "b", "l", "e", "list"]
>>> string_list[-1]
'list'
>>> string_list[-2]
'e'
>>> string_list[-6]
't'
```

Slicing Lists

The slicing operator [:] is used to access a range of list elements.

For example:

```
letter_list = ["P", "y", "t", "h", "o", "n", "P", "r", "o", "g", "r",
"a", "m"]
```

```
>>> letter_list[0:6]
['P', 'y', 't', 'h', 'o', 'n']

>>> letter_list[6:]
['P', 'r', 'o', 'g', 'r', 'a', 'm']

>>> letter_list[2:9]
['t', 'h', 'o', 'n', 'P', 'r', 'o']

>>> letter_list[:-3]
['P', 'y', 't', 'h', 'o', 'n', 'P', 'r', 'o', 'g']

>>> letter_list[:]
['P', 'y', 't', 'h', 'o', 'n', 'P', 'r', 'o', 'g', 'r', 'a', 'm']
```

Adding Elements to a List

Unlike strings, a list is mutable. This means that after creating a list, you can add, modify, or delete an item. To add an item to list, you can use either the append() or the extend() method.

The append() method

The append() method is used when you want to add a single item to the end of a list.

The syntax is:

list_name.append(a)

The extend() method

The extend() method is used when you want to add two or more items to a list.

The syntax is:

list_name.extend(L)

To illustrate how these two methods are used, create a list of numbers:

num_list =[10, 20, 30, 40, 50]

To add the number 100 to the list:

>>> num_list.append(100)

Now, display the updated list:

>>> num_list
[10, 20, 30, 40, 50, 100]

The number 100 has been added to the end of num_list.

Assuming you want to add a list of numbers (5, 15, 25, 35, 45, 55) to num_list, you have to use the extend() method:

>>> num_list.extend([5, 15, 25, 35, 45, 55])

Now, display the updated num_list:

>>> num_list
[10, 20, 30, 40, 50, 100, 5, 15, 25, 35, 45, 55]

The numbers have been added to the end of the list.

Inserting Item(s) to a List

The methods append() and extend() both add element(s) at the end of a list. There are times, however, when you need to place an item on a specific location on a list. Python's insert() method can be used to insert an item on a desired position.

The syntax is:

list_name.insert(index, object)

The index specifies the intended location of the item to be inserted while object refers to the new item.

To illustrate, create a list named even_num:

>>> even_num = [2, 10, 12, 16, 18, 20]

Assuming you want to insert the number 14 between 12, and 16, its index number will be 4. Hence, to place 14 on index 4:

>>>even_num.insert(3, 14)   # index 3, object 14

Now, type even_num to display the modified even_num list:

>>> even_num
[2, 10, 12, 14, 16, 18, 20]

Changing Elements of a List

To change an item or a range of items on a list, you will use the assignment (=) and indexing [] operators.

For example, here is a list with an odd item:

>>> colors = ["red", "blue","yellow", "beige", "slacks", "green"]

The string "slacks" does not belong to a list of colors and you want to replace it with the color "orange".

You can do that by accessing the index of slacks and assigning it to "orange":

>>> colors[4] = "orange"

To display the modified list, type colors:

>>> colors
['red', 'blue', 'yellow', 'beige', 'orange', 'green']

The string "slacks" had been replaced by "orange".

Assuming you want to replace the colors yellow, beige, and orange with another list of colors, you can specify an index range to replace multiple values at once instead of changing the items individually.

For example, to replace the color strings on index 2 to 4 with the color strings purple, pink, and maroon:

>>> colors[2:5] = ['purple', 'pink', 'maroon']

Now, type colors to display the modified colors list:

>>> colors
['red', 'blue', 'purple', 'pink', 'maroon', 'green']

Concatenating Lists

You can use the + operator to concatenate or combine two or more lists.

To illustrate, create three lists with the following items:

```
>>> list_1 = ['x', 'y', 'z']
>>> list_2 = [5, 10, 15]
>>> list_3 = ['soccer', 'basketball', 'baseball']
```

Next concatenate the list using the + operator:

```
>>> list_1 + list_2 + list_3
```

The statement will return a combined list of all items:

```
['x', 'y', 'z', 5, 10, 15, 'soccer', 'basketball', 'baseball']
```

Repeating a List

To repeat a list, you will use the * operator and a number to specify the number of times you want the list to be repeated.

For example, to repeat the list ['one', 'two', 'three'] three times:

```
>>> ['one', 'two', 'three']* 3
['one', 'two', 'three', 'one', 'two', 'three', 'one', 'two', 'three']
```

Here's another way to do it:

```
>>> list_a = ['one', 'two', 'three']
```

>>> list_a * 3
['one', 'two', 'three', 'one', 'two', 'three', 'one', 'two', 'three']

Removing or Deleting Items

The methods remove() and pop() can be used to remove an item from a list.

The remove() method:

The remove() method is used to delete a specific item while the pop() method is used to remove an item at a specified index or the last item if the index is not supplied.

Syntax:

list_name.remove(object)

For example, create a list and name it letters:

>>> letters = ['a', 'b', 'c', 'd', 'D', 8, 'e', 'f', 10.5]

The list contains items that do not belong to the list, namely 8 and 10.5. You can use the remove() method to delete the two items individually :

>>> letters.remove(8)
>>> letters.remove(10.5)

To display the updated list:

>>> letters
['a', 'b', 'c', 'd', 'D', 'e', 'f']

The pop() method

The pop() method is used to delete the item associated with a specific index. If the user does not supply an index, pop() removes and returns the last item on the list.

Syntax:

list_name.pop(index)

To illustrate, you can use the list letter in the above example:

>>> letters
['a', 'b', 'c', 'd', 'D', 'e', 'f']

The letter list contains a capitalized letter D which can be removed using pop() by indicating its index.

For example:

>>> letters.pop(4)
'D'

To display the updated letters list:

>>> letters
['a', 'b', 'c', 'd', 'e', 'f']

If you want to delete the last item on the list using pop(), you should not supply an index. For example:

>>> letters.pop()
'f'

To view the modified list:

```
>>> letters
['a', 'b', 'c', 'd', 'e']
```

Emptying a List

You can use the clear() method to empty a list.

Syntax:

list_name.clear()

For example, to clear the letters list:

```
>>> letters.clear()
```

Here's the updated letters list:
```
>>> letters
[]
```

Deleting Items Using the Keyword del

The keyword del can be used to delete one or more items on a list or the entire list itself.

Syntax:

```
del list_name[]        #deletes a single item
del list_name[:]       #deletes a range of items
```

For example, create a new list:

```
>>> new_list = ['b', 'e', 'g', 'i', 'n', 'n', 'e', 'r']
```

Delete the item on index 4, letter n:

>>> del new_list[4]

To view the updated list:

>>> new_list
['b', 'e', 'g', 'i', 'n', 'e', 'r']

To delete the entire list:

>>> del new_list   #deletes the list

Another way to delete a range of items is by assigning an empty list to the indicated slice of items that you want to remove.

To illustrate, create a list named integer_list:

>>> integer_list = [1, 3, 5, 7, 9, 12, 2.5, 'age', 8.5, 15, 18]

Delete the items on index 6 to 9 by replacing them with an empty list:

>>> integer_list[6:9] = []

To display the updated list:

>>> integer_list
[1, 3, 5, 7, 9, 12, 15, 18]

You can also delete all list items by specifying the entire range of items and assigning an empty space:

>>> integer_list[:] = []

To view the modified list:

>>> integer_list
[]

Sorting Items on a List

The sort() method is used to sort list items of similar data types in ascending order.

Syntax:

list_name.sort()

To illustrate the sort() method, create these two lists:

>>>list_1 = [20, 5,10, 30, 15, 25]
>>> list_a = ['x', 'y', 'z', 'a', 'b', 'c']

Use the sort() method and print both lists:

>>> list_1.sort()
>>> print(list_1)
[5, 10, 15, 20, 25, 30]

>>> list_a.sort()
>>> print(list_a)
['a', 'b', 'c', 'x', 'y', 'z']

The items in both lists are now arranged in ascending order. To view the items in the reverse or descending order, you will have to use Python's reverse method.

Syntax:

list_name.reverse()

Applying the reverse() method to list_1 and list_a:
>>> list_1.reverse()
>>> print(list_1)
[30, 25, 20, 15, 10, 5]

>>> list_a.reverse()
>>> print(list_a)
['z', 'y', 'x', 'c', 'b', 'a']

The sort() method can only be used to arrange items of similar data type. Python will raise a TypeError every time you attempt to sort a mixed list.

Tuple

A tuple is an immutable sequence type that contains an ordered collection of objects. A tuple can hold mixed types of data and can hold as many items as needed.

How to Create a Tuple

To create a tuple, you will generally enclose tuple items inside parentheses and separate them with comma.

Examples:

```
mytuple_a = ("a", "Joseph", "dreamer")     #strings
mytuple_one = (12, 2.5, 17, 10.4, 6.2, 98.5))     #numeric
mytuple_y = ("news", 16, 2,5)     #mixed-type
```

Accessing Tuple Items

To access items on a tuple, you can use indexing and slicing.

Indexing

Earlier, you have learned how to access characters in a string and items in a list through indexing. You will use the same steps to access items in a tuple. The index operator is used to indicate the index of the element you want to access. The first element takes index zero.

To illustrate, create new_tuple with strings as elements:

new_tuple = ('p', 'r', 'o', 'g', 'r', 'a', 'm', 'm', 'e', 'r')

To access the first element on the tuple:

>>> new_tuple[0]
'p'

To access the 7th element:

>>> new_tuple[7]
'm'

To access the 6th element:

>>> new_tuple[6]
'm'

>>> new_tuple
('p', 'r', 'o', 'g', 'r', 'a', 'm', 'm', 'e', 'r')

Negative Indexing

Because it is a sequence type, you can access tuples through negative indexing. The last item takes the -1 index, the penultimate item the -2 index, and so on.

```
>>> new_tuple[-1]
'r'
>>> new_tuple[-7]
'g'
```

Slicing a Tuple

Slicing a tuple allows you to access several items at the same time. To do this, you can use the slicing operator (:).

To illustrate how you can slice a range of items, create a_tuple:

```
>>> a_tuple = ('w', 'e', '6', 'm', '7', 13)
```

To access the elements from the 2nd to the 5th index:
```
>>> a_tuple[2:6]
('l', 'm', '7', 13)
```

```
>>> a_tuple[3:]
('m', '7', 13)
```

Sets

A set is an unordered collection of unique elements. A set is mutable but its elements should be immutable. Sets are used to perform math operations such as intersection, union, or symmetric difference.

Creating a Set

You can create a set by enclosing all items in curly braces {} and assigning it to a variable. You can also create a set with set(), a built-in function. A set can store items of varying data types such as a type, string, or integers but it cannot hold mutable elements such as a dictionary, set, or list.

Python does not allow duplicate elements within a set. When you create a set, the interpreter evaluates the set and removes duplicate items.

For example, try entering a set creation statement, my_set, which contains duplicate elements:

>>> my_set = {'apple', 'peach', 'grape', 'apple', 'strawberry', 'grape'}

Now, access my_set to view its elements:

>>> my_set
{'peach', 'grape', 'apple', 'strawberry'}

Python simply removed duplicate set elements and saved the set without them.

Try entering a set with duplicate items on the prompt and watch how Python returns the set without the duplicate content:

>>> {18, 0, 6, 5, 14, 18, 12, 5}
{0, 5, 6, 12, 14, 18}

Here's how to create a set with the set() function:

```
>>>       set(['apple',    'mango',    'pear',    'pineapple',
'banana','apple', 'pear'])
{'apple', 'pineapple', 'pear', 'banana', 'mango'}
```

Notice that Python also removed duplicate items.

To create an empty set, you can use the set() function without an argument. You cannot create an empty set with curly braces as this is reserved for creating an empty dictionary.

```
>>> empty_set = set()
>>> type(empty_set)
<class 'set'>
```

Adding Elements to a Set

Because sets are mutable, you can modify, add, replace, or remove their elements. You cannot use indexing or slicing to access the elements because sets are unordered. Instead, you can use the methods add() or update() to change set elements. The add() method is used to append a single item to a set. The update() method is used to add multiple elements. You can use strings, tuples, list, or another set as argument with the update() method.

For example:

```
>>> odd_set = {1, 3, 5, 7, 9, 11, 13}
```

To add an element, 15, to odd_set, you will use the add() method:

```
>>> odd_set.add(15)
>>> odd_set
{1, 3, 5, 7, 9, 11, 13, 15}
```

To add a list to odd_set, you will use the update() method:

```
>>> odd_set.update(['a', 'c', 'e', 'g', 'i'])
>>> odd_set
{1, 3, 5, 7, 9, 11, 'e', 13, 15, 'g', 'i', 'c', 'a'}
```

Removing Set Elements

Using remove() and discard() methods

To remove a specific item from a set, you can use either the remove() or discard() method. If you specify a non-existent element for removal, the remove() method will raise a KeyError while the discard() method will simply retain the original set.

For example, create a set and name it letter_set:

```
>>>letter_set = {'a', 'b', 'c', 'd', 'e', 'f', 'g'}
```

Use remove() and discard() to remove the letters 'b' and 'g' individually:

```
>>> letter_set.remove('b')
>>> letter_set
{'d', 'e', 'g', 'f', 'c', 'a'}

>>> letter_set.discard('g')
>>> letter_set
{'d', 'e', 'f', 'c', 'a'}
```

The pop() method

The pop() method is another way to remove an item on a set. This method removes a random element and returns the removed item.

To illustrate, create birds_set:

```
>>> birds_set = {'Parrot', 'Jay', 'Mockingbird', 'Kingfisher', 'Owl'}
```

Use the pop() method to remove a random element:

```
>>> birds_set.pop()
'Kingfisher'
>>> birds_set
{'Parrot', 'Mockingbird', 'Owl', 'Jay'}
```

The clear() method

The clear() method is used to remove the entire elements of a set:

To remove all elements of birds_set:

```
>>> birds_set.clear()
>>> birds_set
set()
```

Set Operations

Python supports different types of set operations such as set union, intersection, difference, and symmetric difference.

Set Union

A union of two sets is a set that contains all elements of the given sets. You can use the | operator or the union() method to implement this set operation. The output is a combination of all elements which are arranged in ascending order.

Create the sets X and Y:

>>> X = {'square', 'rectangle', 'triangle', 'circle', 'oval'}
>>> Y = {'sphere','cone', 'cylinder', 'cube', 'pyramid'}

Combine two sets using the | operator:

>>> X|Y
{'pyramid', 'triangle', 'circle', 'rectangle', 'cone', 'oval', 'cylinder', 'square', 'sphere', 'cube'}

Now, use the union()method to combine the elements of X and Y and return the combined elements in ascending order:

>>> X.union(Y)
{'pyramid', 'triangle', 'circle', 'rectangle', 'cone', 'oval', 'cylinder', 'square', 'sphere', 'cube'}

You will get similar results if you choose to use X as argument:

>>> Y.union(X)
{'pyramid', 'triangle', 'square', 'circle', 'cone', 'rectangle', 'oval', 'cylinder', 'sphere', 'cube'}

Set Intersection

Set intersection refers to a set containing elements that are common to two given sets. You will use either the & operator or the intersection() method to implement this set operation. Both will return a set with common elements.

Example:

```
>>> a = {'p', 'r', 'o', 'b', 'l', 'e', 'm'}
>>> b = {'p', 'r', 'e', 'v', 'i' 'o', 'u', 's'}
```

& operator:

```
>>> a & b
{'r', 'e', 'p'}
```

intersection() method:

```
>>> a.intersection(b)
{'r', 'e', 'p'}
```

or:

```
>>> b.intersection(a)
{'r', 'e', 'p'}
```

Set Difference

Set difference is a set of elements that can be found in one set but not in another set. The set difference operation is implemented with either the – operator or the difference() method.

For example:

Create two sets a and b:

```
>>> a = {'m', 'a', 'r', 'k', 'e', 't'}
>>> b = {'s', 't', 'o', 'r','e'}
```

The difference between sets a and b (a − b) is a set of elements that are found in set a but not in set b:

```
>>> a - b
{'a', 'k', 'm'}
```

You will get the same output if you use the difference() method:
```
>>> a.difference(b)
{'a', 'k', 'm'}
```

On the other hand, the difference between sets b and a (b-a) is a set of elements that can be found in set b but not in set a:

```
>> y - x
{'s', 'o'}
```

You will have similar results if you use the difference method:

```
>>> b.difference(a)
{'s', 'o'}
```

Set Symmetric Difference

Symmetric deference is a set of elements that are not common between two sets. It is implemented with either the ^ operator or symmetric_difference() method.

For example, create two sets a and b:

```
>>> a = {5, 10, 15, 20, 25}
>>> b = {10, 20, 30, 40, 50}
```

The following expressions yield the same result:

```
>>> a ^ b
{5, 40, 15, 50, 25, 30}

>>> b ^ a
{5, 40, 15, 50, 25, 30}


>>> a.symmetric_difference(b)
{5, 40, 15, 50, 25, 30}

>>> b.symmetric_difference(a)
{5, 40, 15, 50, 25, 30}
```

Dictionary

A Python dictionary is a container for a collection of unordered key-value pairs. The keys and values are separated by a colon (:) and all pairs are enclosed within curly braces {}. The keys of a dictionary are immutable and can only be a number, tuple, or string. The values, however, are mutable and may contain any data type. You can only access dictionary values by accessing its keys.

A dictionary is a highly useful container in Python. It allows programmers to save, manage, and retrieve data using a key-value structure that is commonly used in menus, phone books, directories, and similar registries.

Creating a dictionary

To create an empty dictionary, you will use the syntax:

dict = {}

To create a dictionary with key-value pairs:

```
dict  =  {key1:value1,  key2:value2,  key_3:value3,
key4:value4}
```

Accessing the Elements of a Dictionary

A dictionary is an unordered data type. Hence, you cannot use the indexing operator to access the values. You will have to use the key if you need to access the associated value. To do this, you can either place a specific key inside square brackets or apply the get() method.

For example, here is a dictionary with key:value pairs:

member_1 = {'Name':'Sheryll Storm', 'Age':24, 'Telephone No.':1866432185}

To access the values stored in the member_1 dictionary:

```
>>> member_1['Name']
'Sheryll Storm'

>>> member_1['Age']
24

>>> member_1['Telephone No.']
1866432185
```

To access the dictionary values using the get() method:

```
>>> member_1.get('Name')
'Sheryll Storm'

>>> member_1.get('Age')
24

>>> member_1.get('Telephone No.')
```

1866432185

Adding and Modifying Dictionary Entries

Adding Dictionary Entries

To add a new key-value pair or modify the values of a dictionary, you will use the assignment (=) operator. Python evaluates the new entry and checks if there is a similar key in the current dictionary. If there is none, then it appends the key:value pair. If the key already exists, then it updates the value of the existing key.

The syntax for adding a dictionary entry is:

dict_name[key] = b

For instance, if you want to add a key-value pair to the member_1 dictionary, you can use this expression:

member_1['sex'] = 'female'

Now, view the updated dictionary:

```
>>> member_1
{'sex': 'female', 'Age': 24, 'Telephone No.': 1866432185,
'Name': 'Sheryll Storm'}
```

You can add more key-value pairs to member_1:

```
>>> member_1['Position'] = 'Secretary'
>>> member_1['Department'] = 'Finance'
```

To display the updated data of member_1 dictionary:

```
>>> member_1
{'Position': 'Secretary', 'Department': 'Finance', 'sex': 'female', 'Telephone No.': 1866432185, 'Age': 24, 'Name': 'Sheryll Storm'}
```

Modifying Dictionary Values

To modify the current value of a dictionary key, you can use the assignment operator to specify the new value that you want to associate with a key. For example, if you want to modify the position from 'Secretary' to 'Supervisor' in member_1 dictionary, you can use the statement:

```
>>> member_1['Position'] = 'Supervisor'
```

To view the updated member_1 dictionary:

```
>>> member_1
{'Position': 'Supervisor', 'Department': 'Finance', 'sex': 'female', 'Telephone No.': 1866432185, 'Age': 24, 'Name': 'Sheryll Storm'}
```

Removing or Deleting Entries from a Dictionary

Using the pop() method:

You can use the pop() method to remove a key-value pair from a dictionary. This method removes the specified data pair and returns the value of the deleted key.

For example:

```
>>> menu = {'carbonara':5.75, 'spaghetti':5.50, 'pizza':
6.00, 'garlic bread':1.75, 'meatballs':3.25, 'fried
mushrooms':5.85}
```

To remove the key entry 'fried mushrooms':

```
>>> menu.pop('fried mushrooms')
5.85
```

To view the updated menu dictionary:

```
>>> menu
{'garlic bread': 1.75, 'pizza': 6.0, 'meatballs': 3.25,
'carbonara': 5.75, 'spaghetti': 5.5}
```

The popitem() method

The popitem() method is used to remove a random key-value pair from a dictionary. The method does not take an argument and returns the deleted key-value pair.

For example, you can use the popitem method on the menu dictionary with the statement:

```
>>> menu.popitem()
('garlic bread', 1.75)
```

To view the updated menu dictionary:

```
>>> menu
{'pizza': 6.0, 'meatballs': 3.25, 'carbonara': 5.75, 'spaghetti':
5.5}
```

The clear() method

The clear() method is used to remove all key-value pairs in a dictionary:

For example, to remove the remaining entries in the menu dictionary:

>>> menu.clear()

To view the updated menu:
>>> menu
{}

Removing all key-value pairs leaves you an empty dictionary.

Deleting a Dictionary

The del keyword is used to delete a dictionary.

The syntax is:

del dict_name

For example, to delete the menu dictionary:

del menu

Python provides other useful methods for working with a dictionary.

item() method

The item() method returns a list of key-values stored in a dictionary.

syntax: dict.items()

Example:

>>> stud1 = {'Quiz':98, 'Homework':95, 'Recitation':89, 'Test':95}

>>> stud1.items()
dict_items([('Test', 95), ('Homework', 95), ('Quiz', 98), ('Recitation', 89)])

keys() method

The keys() method is used to return a list of keys in a dictionary.

syntax: dict.keys()

Example:

This will use the dictionary stud1 created above:

>>> stud1.keys()
dict_keys(['Test', 'Homework', 'Quiz', 'Recitation'])

values() method

The values() method returns a list of all dictionary values.

syntax: dict.values()

For example, to return the values of stud1 dictionary:

>>> stud1.values()
dict_values([95, 95, 98, 89])

Using the dict() function to create a new dictionary

dict() is a built-in function that can be used to create a new dictionary from a list of tuple pairs.

To illustrate, create a list of tuple pairs:

```
>>> pairs = [("rooster", "hen"), ("bull", "cow"), ("dog", "bitch"), ("jack", "jenny"), ("buck", "doe")]
```

Convert the pairs list to a dictionary using the dict() function and store the dictionary elements in pairs_dict:

```
>>> pairs_dict = dict(pairs)
```

Use type() to view the data typeof pairs_dict:

```
>>> type(pairs_dict)
<class 'dict'>
```

Boolean Data Type

There are two Boolean data types: True or False. These two values are used when evaluating comparisons, conditional expressions, and in other structures that require values representation for True or False.

To illustrate how Boolean data types are used, you can create three variables to hold Boolean values derived from assigned expressions.

Python

```
>>> bool_1 = (18 >= 5)        #18 is greater than or
equal to 5
>>> bool_2 = (15 == 3*8)      #15 is equal to the
product of 3 times 8
>>> bool_3 = (12 != 3*5)      #12 is not equal to the
product of 3 times 5
```

Use the print function to view the values of each variable:

```
>>> print(bool_1)
>>> print(bool_2)
>>> print(bool_3)
True
False
True
```

Chapter 5: Python Operators

Operators are symbols that signify the execution of a specific process. Python provides several types of operators:

- Arithmetic Operators
- Assignment Operators
- Relational Operators
- Logical Operators
- Identity Operators
- Membership Operators
- Bitwise Operators

Arithmetic Operators

Arithmetic operators are used to perform mathematical operations in Python.

Python supports 7 arithmetic operators:

Addition	+
Subtraction	-
Multiplication	*
Division	/
Exponent	**
Modulos	%
Floor Division	//

Addition (+)

The addition operator adds the value of the left and right operands.

```
>>>12 + 4
```

16

Subtraction (-)

The subtraction operators subtracts the value of the right operand from that of the left operand.

```
>>>13 − 4
9
```

Multiplication (*)

The multiplication operator multiplies the left and right operands.

```
>>>12 * 3
36
```

Division (/)

The division operator divides the left operand by the value of the right operand.

```
>>>12 / 4
3.0
```

Exponent (**)

The exponent operator raises the base number to the power signified by the number after the operator.

```
>>> 4**2
16
```

Modulos (%)

The modulos operator returns the remainder after performing a division operation of the left operand with the right operand.

```
>>> 20 % 6
2
```

Floor Division (//)

The floor division operator performs a division operation, drops the fractional part, and returns the quotient as a whole number.

```
>>> 20 // 3
6
```

Assignment Operators

Assignment operators are used to assign values to variables.

= Operator

The = operator assigns the right operand to the left operand.

Examples:

```
x = 35
a = b
```

```
vowel_list = ['a', 'e', 'i', 'o', 'u']
new_dict    =    {'Name':'Brandon    Smart',    'Age':25,
'Employment Status: ':'Regular'}
x = 2 * 4
```

Python supports multiple assignments in a single statement:

```
a, b, c = "Polar bear", 12, 5.5
```
Python likewise allows the assignment of one value to a several variables in a single statement:

```
a = b = c = "high cube"
num = item = sum = 27
```

add and +=

The 'add and' operator adds the value of the left and right operands and assigns the total to the left operand.

```
x += 4
y += x
```

subtract and -=

The 'subtract and' operator subtracts the value of the right operand from that of the left and assigns the difference to the left number.

```
x -= y
a -= 4
```

multiply and *=

The 'multiply and' operator multiplies the left and right operands and assigns the product to the left operand.

x *= z
a *= 4

divide and /=

The 'divide and' operator divides the value of the left operand with the right operand and assigns the result to the left operand.

x /= c
y /= 4

modulos and %=

The 'modulos and' operator divides the value of the left operand with the right
operand then assigns the remainder to the left.

x %= a
x %= 3

floor division and //=

The 'floor division and' operator performs a floor division of the left operand by the right operand and assigns the result to the left operand.

x //= a
x //= 2

Relational or Comparison Operators

Relational operators evaluate a comparative expression and returns either True or False.

Python provides the following relational operators:

Operator	Meaning
>	is greater than
<	is less than
==	is equal to
!=	is not equal to
>=	is greater than or equal to
<=	is less than or equal to

Examples:

```
>>> 25 == 5*2*3
False

>>> 3*4 <= 3*2*3
True

>>> 45 >= (15*5)
False

>>> 36 != 3**2*4
False

>>> (12*3) > 30
True

>>> 30 < (3*15)
True
```

Logical Operators

Python provides three kinds of logical operators:

or
and
not

Python evaluates expressions with logical operators by applying the following tests:

x = first argument, y = second argument

x or y   if x is true, it returns True. If x is false, it evaluates y and returns the result as either True or False. In other words, only one argument needs to be True for the expression to return True.

Examples:

>>> (24>9) or (12<9)   #The   first argument is true.
True

>>> (7 > 14) or (5 < 15)   #The second argument is true.
True

x and y   If x is true, it evaluates y. If y is true, it returns True. If y is false, it returns False. If x is false, it returns False. In other words, both arguments should be true in order for the operation to return True.

Examples:

```
>>> (12>23) and (25>10)              #    The     first
argument is false.
False

>>> (15 == 3*5) and (15 < 3**4)        #Both arguments
are true.
True
```

not x   If x is true, it returns False. Otherwise, it returns True.

Examples:

```
>>> not (5*4 > 20)
True

>>> not (15 > 4**3)
True
```

Identity Operators

Identity operators check if the given objects are stored on the same memory location. There are two identity operators in Python: is and is not.

is   returns True if the specified variables refer to the same object and returns False if otherwise.

is not returns False if the specified variables refer to the same object or memory location and True if otherwise.

Examples:

```
>>> a = 12
>>> b = 12
```

```
>>> a is b
True
```

The variables a and b contains integers of similar value which makes them identical and equal.

```
>>> x = 'immutable'
>>> y = 'immutable'
>>> x is not y
False
```

The variables x and hold the same string and data type and are identical and equal. Hence, the 'is not' identity operator returned False.

```
>>> list_a = [12, 24, 36]
>>> list_b = [12, 24, 36]
>>> list_a is list_b
False
```

The variables list_a and list_b contain the same elements and are equal. However, they are not identical because lists are mutable and are thus saved separately in memory. Hence, the id operator 'is' returned False.

Membership Operators

Membership operators are used to check for the occurrence of a value or variable in sequence types like list, tuple, set, or string. You can use the membership operator on a dictionary but you can only test for the existence of a key in the given dictionary, not its value. Python supports two membership operators: in and not in.

in   returns True if the value or variable occurs in a specified sequence and returns False if otherwise not in   returns True if the value or variable is not found in a specified sequence and returns False if otherwise

Examples:

```
>>> a_string = 'Hello, World!'
>>> 'W' in a_string
True
```

```
>>> my_dict = {'color': 'silver', 'brand': 'Benches', 'model':'No go'}
>>> 'brand' in my_dict
True
>>> 'silver' in my_dict          #silver is a value, not a key.
False
```

Chapter 6:Built-in Functions

Python has numerous built-in functions and modules that you can access readily to make useful programs quickly, easily, and efficiently.

Here is a table of built-in functions:

abs()	any()	ascii()
all()	bool()	bin()
bytes()	bytearray()	callable()
compile()	chr()	classmethod()
dir()	delattr()	complex()
dict()	divmod()	enumerate()
eval()	exec()	filter()
float()	format()	frozenset()
global()	getattr()	hasattr()
hash()	help()	hex()
__import__()	id()	int ()
input()	issubclass()	isinstance()
iter()	len()	list()
locals()	map()	max()
min()	memoryview()	next()
object()	oct()	open()
ord()	pow()	print()
property()	range()	repr()
round()	reversed()	set()
slice()	setattr()	sorted()
sum()	str()	staticmethod()
super()	type()	tuple()
vars()	zip()	

max()

The max() function returns the largest value among the given arguments.

Syntax: max(x, y, z)

Examples:

```
>>> max(-24, 5, 20)
20

>>>max(1, -100, 0, -30)
1
```

len()

The len() function returns the size, length, or the number of items of a given data.
Examples:

```
>>> a = "program"
>>> len(a)
7

>>> my_list = ['box', 'ball', 'spring', 'cards', 'rabbit', 'hat',
'coat', 'cane']
>>> len(my_list)
8

>>> my_dict = {'key1': 12, 'key2':20, 'key3':10, 'key4':60}
>>> len(my_dict)
4
```

abs()

The abs() function returns the absolute value of integers or floats. The value returned is a positive number.

Examples:

```
>>> abs(-15)
15

>>> abs(25)
25

>>>abs(-130)
130
```

min()

The min() function returns the smallest value among the given arguments.

Syntax:

```
min(x, y, z)
```

Examples:

```
>>> min(14, -15, 1)
-15

>>> min(3, 18, 1, 0)
0
```

type()

The type() function returns the data type of the argument.

Examples:

```
>>> type("Python")
<class 'str'>

>>> type(28)
<class 'int'>

>>> type(50.5)
<class 'float'>

>>> type(2 +4j)
<class 'complex'>
```

sum()

The function sum() returns the total value of items on a specified list.

Example:

```
>>> my_numbers = [2, 4, 6, 8, 10, 12, 14, 16]
>>> sum(my_numbers)
72
```

round()

The round() function returns a rounded number:

Syntax:

round(x[,n])   where x is the number to be rounded and n is the number of digits to the right of the decimal point.

```
>>> round(1769.54678, 2)
1769.55
```

```
>>> round(234392.9876543212345, 4)
234392.9877
>>> round(2352353.9830)
2352354
```

Notice that when the decimal digit is not specified, rounding defaults to zero decimal places.

The range() function

The range() function is used to create a list of numbers containing arithmetic progressions. It is most commonly used in 'for loops'. Its syntax is range(start, end, step). If only one argument is given, this is assumed to be the end of the range. If the start argument is omitted, the range starts at the default value of zero. If the step argument is omitted, the progression default value of 1 is used.

The use of the range() function generates an iterator which progresses a list of integers from a default or given value to an ending value.

To illustrate, enter range(15) on the prompt:

```
>>> range(15)
range(0, 15)
```

To view the numbers on the specified range, you can make a list out of the range with the list keyword:

```
>>> list(range(15))
[0, 1, 2, 3, 4, 5, 6, 7, 8, 9, 10, 11, 12, 13, 14]
```

Take note that since no starting value was given, the range started at zero. Since no progression was given, the default progression of 1 was used. The ending value of 15 was given and this meant that the last number on the range is 14 which is one less than the ending argument of 15.

Here is a range() expression containing 3 arguments:

```
>>> range(1, 30, 3)
range(1, 30, 3)

>>> list(range(1, 30, 3))
[1, 4, 7, 10, 13, 16, 19, 22, 25, 28]
```

Since 1 was the specified starting number, the list started at 1 with a progression of 3. The last integer on the series, 28, is the last number on the progression before the specified ending of 30.

If you use zero as the starting number on the range, you would have this list instead:

```
>>> list(range(0,30,3))
[0, 3, 6, 9, 12, 15, 18, 21, 24, 27]
```

The input() Function

Python offers a built-in input() function to obtain user's input from the keyboard. The input() function has an optional parameter, a prompt string, which is displayed onscreen whenever the function is called. The program stops to wait for user's keyboard entry and displays it onscreen.

For example, here is a sample program that prompts for the user's name and age:

```
id = input("Please enter your First Name: ")
print("Good day", id + "!")
age = int(input("Please enter your age.: "))
print("Thank you, " + id + "." + " So you are",  str(age),
      "years old. Cool!")
```

Run the program and enter Micah as first name and 15 as age. You will get this output:

```
Please enter your First Name: Micah
Good day Micah!
Please enter your age.: 15
Thank you, Micah. So you are 15 years old. Cool!
```

The print() Function

The print() function facilitates the display of data on screen, the default output device.

Syntax:

print()

Examples:

```
>>> print("It's easy to print in Python.")
It's easy to print in Python.

>>> print(2*3)
6

>>> print(4**3)
64

>>> x = 50
>>> print('The value of x is', x )
The value of x is 50
```

You can print several variables in one print statement by positional formatting:

```
x = 12
y = "high school"
z = "student"

print("I am a " + str(x), "year-old", y, z + ".")
```

Here's the output:

I am a 12 year-old high school student.

Using the str.format() method

The str.format() method is used to control output when printing string objects.

By default, values are displayed based on their position as argument in the format statement. If you prefer this printing arrangement, you can use curly braces {} as place holders for values in the print parameters.

For example:

```
>>> x = 20; y=50; z = 80

>>> print('The value of x is {}, y is {}, and z is {}.'.format(x, y, z))
The value of x is 20, y is 50, and z is 80.
```

If you want the values to appear in a different order, you will have to supply an index number inside the curly braces to indicate the index of the value that you want to appear in that position. Indexing starts from zero so the first value gets the index 0, the second gets index 1, and so on.

Using the same example, you can change the order of appearance of values:

```
>>> x = 20; y=50; z = 80
>>> print("The value of z is {2}, y is {1}, and x is {0}.".format(x, y, z))
The value of z is 80, y is 50, and x is 20.
```

You need not always use a variable to format strings for printing. You can use the values themselves as arguments for the format() method.

For example:

```
>>> print('I want {}, {}, {}, and {}!'.format('pizza', 'barbecue', 'carbonara', 'pineapple juice'))
I want pizza, barbecue, carbonara, and pineapple juice!
```

You can also use indexing to change the order of appearance of values:

```
>>> print('I want {1}, {3}, {0}, and {2}!'.format('pizza', 'barbecue', 'carbonara', 'pineapple juice'))
I want barbecue, pineapple juice, pizza, and carbonara!
```

Chapter 7: Flow Control

By default, programs are executed in the sequence in which the statements appear. Flow control structures allow programmers to direct or control the order of program execution. Python supports several conditional statements and loops that you can use when you want your program to perform an action based on the occurrence or non-occurrence of a certain condition.

Conditional Statements

Python supports the following conditional statements:

if statements
if else statements
elif statements
else
nested if...elif...else statements

if statements

An if statement begins with a Boolean expression. This is followed by a statement or a group of statements that specifies the action(s) to be performed if the test expression is evaluated as True.

Syntax:

if test expression
    statement(s)

For example, here's a program snippet that collects keyboard input and uses the input as the basis for subsequent actions.

#This program asks the user to enter a vowel and prints a string based on user's input.

```
vowels = ['a', 'e','i', 'o', 'u', 'A', 'E', 'I', 'O', 'U',]

choice = input("Prove that you are a human by entering a vowel: ")
if choice in vowels:
    print("Thank you. Welcome to humansite.com.")
print("You can only use this site if you are a human being.")
```

Here are possible outputs based on user's response:

In this situation, the user enters letter 'a':

Prove that you are a human by entering a vowel: a
Thank you. Welcome to humansite.com.
You can only use this site if you are a human being.

This time, the user enters letter h, a non-vowel:

Prove that you are a human by entering a vowel: h
You can only use this site if you are a human being.

Notice that in the second situation, the program did not print the statement under the 'if' test expression. This statement is only printed when the user enters a vowel which will make the condition True.

if...else statements

An if...else conditional statement starts with an 'if' test expression just like the 'if' structure. If the response is True, then Python will execute the code block under the 'if statement'. If the expression tests as False, Python will execute the statements in the 'else' block.

syntax:

```
if test expression:
    statement block
else:
    statement block
```

Here's an example of a program with an 'if...else' structure:

```
#This program checks if a product is on stock and prints
the appropriate string.

stocks = ['pen', 'pencil', 'sharpener', 'stationery', 'marker',
'highlighters']

item = input("Please enter your order: ")
if item in stocks:
    print("Thank you. Please pay at the counter.")
else:
    print("Sorry", item  + " is out of stock at the moment.")
```

Run the program and type 'marker' at the prompt:

Please enter your order: marker
Thank you. Please pay at the counter.

Now, type mouse, a non-existent item in stocks:

Please enter your order: mouse

Sorry mouse is out of stock at the moment.

if...elif...else statements

An if...elif...else structure facilitates the use of multiple test expressions in programs. The 'if' statement first checks if the test expression is true. If True, it executes the statements under the 'if' block. If False, it runs the test expression in the 'elif' (else if) line. If True, it executes the statements in the elif block. If False, control passes to the 'else' block. Take note that an if...elif...else structure can have as many elif blocks as required but can only have one 'else' block.

Syntax:

```
if test condition:
    if block
elif test condition:
    elif block
else:
    else block
```

Here's a program with an if...elif...else structure:

```
#This program draws a random number.
#It prints an appropriate string based on the number drawn.


import random                          #random is a built-in Python module

input("Press enter to draw a number. ")
    # get a random number from 1 to 20
number = random.randint(1,20)
print(number)
```

```python
if number > 15:
    print("Welcome to the Bonus Round.")
elif number > 10:
    print("You may draw another number.")
elif number > 5:
    print("You may join next quarter's edition of
Luckystakes.")
else:
    print("Thank you for joining the game. Better luck next
year.")
```

When you run the program repeatedly, you will run into different scenarios depending on the random number returned by the program:

Press enter to draw a number.
16
Welcome to the Bonus Round.

Press enter to draw a number.
14
You may draw another number.

Press enter to draw a number.
8
You may join next quarter's edition of Luckystakes.

Press enter to draw a number.
20
Welcome to the Bonus Round.

Press enter to draw a number.
4

Thank you for joining the game. Better luck next year.

nested if...elif...else statements

Nesting is the practice of organizing data, loop, sequence, or logic structures in layers. Python supports nesting of conditional statement within another conditional statement. You can find this structure in nested if...elif...else statements. Nested conditional statements are useful if you have to check for a sub-condition after the first condition has been evaluated as True. Nesting can go as deep as you need your program to go and is implemented with appropriate indentation.

Syntax:

```
if test_condition1:
   if test_condition1-a:
      statement_block1-a
   elif test_condition1-b:
      statement_block1-b
   else
      statement_block1-c
elif test_condition2:
   statement_block2
else:
   statement_block3
```


Here is a program that uses nested if...elif...else block:

This program asks users to identify themselves as an advertiser or ads viewer
and executes nested conditional statements based on the response given.

```python
choice = int(input("Please enter 1 if you are an advertiser
or 2 if you want to register or log-in as an ads viewer. "))
if choice == 1:
    advert1 = input("Please enter a for new clients and b for
existing clients. ")
    if advert1 == 'a':
        print("Welcome to Pay-Per-Click World.")
    elif advert1 == 'b':
        print("Thank you for your continuous support.")
    else:
        Print("Please check your response.")
elif choice == 2:
    viewer = input("Please enter a to register or b to log-in.
")
    if viewer == 'a':
        name = input("Please enter your name: ")
    elif viewer == 'b':
        print("You may access our log-in page.")
    else:
        print("Please check your response.")
else:
    print("That is not a valid response.")
```

To test how the program responds, run it and provide different responses to the prompt strings. Here are possible results:

Please enter 1 if you are an advertiser or 2 if you want to register or log-in as an ads viewer. 1
Please enter a for new clients and b for existing clients. a
Welcome to Pay-Per-Click World.

Please enter 1 if you are an advertiser or 2 if you want to register or log-in as an ads viewer. 1
Please enter a for new clients and b for existing clients. b
Thank you for your continuous support.

Please enter 1 if you are an advertiser or 2 if you want to register or log-in as an ads viewer. 6
That is not a valid response.

Please enter 1 if you are an advertiser or 2 if you want to register or log-in as an ads viewer. 2
Please enter a to register or b to log-in. a
Please enter your name: Marrie

Please enter 1 if you are an advertiser or 2 if you want to register or log-in as an ads viewer. 2
Please enter a to register or b to log-in. b
You may access our log-in page.

Please enter 1 if you are an advertiser or 2 if you want to register or log-in as an ads viewer. 2
Please enter a to register or b to log-in. 1
Please check your response.

Loops

A loop is a programming control structure that facilitates the repetitive execution of a statement or group of statements.

'for' Loops

A 'for loop' is used to iterate over elements of sequence data types such as strings, tuples, or lists.

Syntax:

```
for val in sequence:
    statement(s)
```

In 'for statements', the variable 'val' stores the value of the elements for each iteration. The loop executes until all items in the sequence are exhausted.

Examples:

for Loop with string:

iterate over a string

```
for letter in 'Python Programming':
    print('<', letter, '>')
```

Run the program and you will get this output:

```
< P >
< y >
< t >
< h >
< o >
< n >
<   >
< P >
< r >
< o >
< g >
< r >
< a >
< m >
< m >
< i >
< n >
< g >
```

for Loop with list

```
#iterate over a list

menu = ['Sushi', 'Sashimi', 'Teriyaki', 'California Maki', 'Udon']

for item in menu:
    print("Delicious, appetizing", item)
```

Run the program and you will have this output:

```
Delicious, appetizing Sushi
Delicious, appetizing Sashimi
Delicious, appetizing Teriyaki
Delicious, appetizing California Maki
Delicious, appetizing Udon
```

for Loop with tuple

```
#for Loop that evaluates if a number in given list is odd or
even
#print the number and tell if it is odd of even

num = (23, 12, 4, 88, 11, 15, 90, 68, 5, 22)

for x in num:
    if x % 2 == 1:
        print(x, "is an odd number.")
    else:
        print(x, "is an even number.")
```

```
23 is an odd number.
12 is an even number.
4 is an even number.
88 is an even number.
11 is an odd number.
```

15 is an odd number.
90 is an even number.
68 is an even number.
5 is an odd number.
22 is an even number.

for loop with the range() function

You can use the range() function to provide the numbers needed by a loop. For instance, if you need the sum of all numbers from 1 to 10:

```
x = 10

total = 0
for num in range(1, x+1):
    total += num

print("Sum of numbers from 1 to %d: %d" % (x, total))
```

If you run the code, this would be your output:
Sum of numbers from 1 to 10: 55   #
1+2+3+4+5+6+7+8+9+10

The while Loop

The 'while loop' is used to control program flow when you need to repeatedly execute a statement or group of statements as long as the test condition is True.

Syntax:

```
while test condition
    statement(s)
```

#program adds number up to num where

```
#num is entered by the user
#total = 1+2+3+4...+num
```

Example:

```
# This program adds numbers up to a certain number.
# The number is entered by the user.
# total = 1+2+3+4+ up to the supplied number

num = int(input("Enter a number: "))

#initialize total and count
total = 0
count = 1

while count <= num:
    total = total + count
    count += 1

#print total
print("The total is: ", total)
```

You should get the following output when you enter 5 and 10:

```
Enter a number: 5
The total is:  15

Enter a number: 10
The total is:  55
```

Break Statement

A break statement is used to end the current loop and instruct Python to execute the statement after the loop.

You can use it to terminate the current iteration, the entire loop, or in any situation that requires immediate exit from the loop. It is commonly used to prevent the execution of the 'else' statement.

Syntax:

```
break
```

#A for loop that terminates once it reaches the item 'pentagon':

```
shapes = ['diamond', 'rectangle', 'circle', 'triangle', 'pentagon', 'sphere']

for item in shapes:
    if item == 'pentagon':
        break
    print(item, "- an amazing shape")
print("Interesting shapes!")
```

Run the program and your output would be:

```
diamond  - an amazing shape
rectangle  - an amazing shape
circle  - an amazing shape
triangle  - an amazing shape
Interesting shapes!
```

Notice that once the shape pentagon is reached, the loop ends and control is passed to the next line after the loop which is a print statement.

Continue Statement

The continue statement is used to skip the remaining statements in the present iteration and directs program flow to the next iteration.

Syntax:

```
continue
```

To illustrate the usage of continue statement, you can replace the break statement in the above example with the continue statement.

```
shapes = ['diamond', 'rectangle', 'circle', 'triangle', 'pentagon', 'sphere']

for item in shapes:
    if item == 'pentagon':
        continue
    print(item, "- an amazing shape")
print("Interesting shapes!")
```

When you run the program, the output would be:

```
diamond  - an amazing shape
rectangle  - an amazing shape
circle  - an amazing shape
triangle  - an amazing shape
sphere  - an amazing shape
Interesting shapes!
```

Notice that when it reached the item 'pentagon', it skipped the iteration and proceeded to the next iteration for the item 'sphere'.

Pass Statement

A pass statement is a null expression. Python will read and execute a pass statement but will not return anything. Pass statements are commonly used as a place holder for programming lines that are required but are yet to be written.

Syntax:
```
pass
```

Examples:

```
#using pass in place of an empty block of code
for y in num_list:
    pass
```

```
#using pass in an empty function block
def my_funct(x):
    pass
```

```
#using pass as placeholder for a class block:
class Employees:
    pass
```

Chapter 8: User-Defined Functions

User-defined functions in Python are blocks of statements that are related. This group of statements performs a user-specified task. Functions facilitate breaking of large complex programs into manageable segments and allow repetition of codes in different parts of the program and across multiple modules. Depending on their usage, functions are variably called methods, procedures, routines, subroutines, or subprograms.

A function is defined with this syntax:

```
def function_name(parameters):
    """docstring"""
    statements
```

A function's definition consists of the following parts:

keyword "def"

A definition statement starts with the keyword "def" which names the function and indicates that the statement is a function header.

function name

The function header statement identifies a function by a unique name which starts in lower case.

parameters

Parameters are optional parts of a function definition which are written inside parentheses. A parameter is used to assign a value to a function.

colon (:)

A colon indicates the end of a function header statement.

docstring

A documentation string is an optional component of a function definition block. It is used to provide information and additional documentation. Simply put, it tells the one reading the Python code what a certain function will do. A docstring is enclosed in triple quotes and is written on the line next to the function header. You can access the docstring by calling the function with __doc__.

statement block

A function's body may consist of one or several valid statements. You must observe the same level of indentation within the block.

return statement

A return statement is used to return the value produced after all the statements in a function have been executed. When no return statement is given, the function returns 'None'.

syntax for a return statement:

return [expression_list]

Here is a simple function with no return statement:

```
def greet(name):
    """Greets the name
    passed as argument."""
    print("Welcome, " + name + ". Have a nice day!")
```


When you run the function with the print statement and provide a name, 'Jayme', as argument, your output would be:

```
>>> print(greet(("Jayme")))
Welcome, Jayme. Have a nice day!
None
```

Notice that since the function did not have a 'return statement' it returned 'None'.

You can access the docstring of the same function by accessing the 'greet' function's __doc__ attribute:

```
>>> greet.__doc__
'Greets the name \n   passed as argument'
```

Likewise, you can access the docstring of the greet function with the print statement:

```
>>> print(greet.__doc__)
Greets the name
  passed as argument
```

Here is a simple function with a return statement:

```
def adder(x, y):
    """Function to get the sum of two numbers."""
    return x + y
```

When run with the print statement and a number combination, the adder function would return the total of the number combination:

```
>>> print(adder(2,5))
7

>>> print(adder(50, 125))
175
```

This function will return a given number's absolute value:

```
def abs_val(num):
    """Returns absolute value
    """
    if num >= 0:
        return num
    else:
        return -num
```

When run with the print() function and a given number, here are examples of what the function would return:

```
>>> print(abs_val(20))
20
>>> print(abs_val(-30))
30
>>> print(abs_val(0))
0
```

This function evaluates if a specified number is an even number:

```
#function to evaluate if a given number
#is an even number
#return the number if even
#otherwise, return a string and None

def even_num(x):
  if x % 2 == 0:
    return x
  else:
    print("Sorry, " + str(x) + " is not an even number.")
```

When used with the print()function, you will get the following output with the numbers 16, 9, and 2:

```
>>> print(even_num(16))
16
```

```
>>> print(even_num(9))
Sorry, 9 is not an even number.
None

>>> print(even_num(2))
2
```

Calling a Function

A function that has been defined can be a valuable component in your program. For it to be useful, however, you have to call the function. There are different ways of calling a function. You can call it through the >>> prompt, through another function, or through a program.

Calling a function through the >>> prompt

The simplest way to call a function is through the Python >>> prompt where you will simply type the function name and the parameters, if any.

To illustrate, here is a function that prints a passed string:

```
def fastprinter(str):                    #prints     passed
string
    print(str)
    return
```

At the >>> prompt, you can call the fastprinter function and supply the argument within the parentheses:

```
>>> fastprinter("I can print any string with fastprinter.")
I can print any string with fastprinter.

>>> fastprinter("1,2,3,a,b,c")
1,2,3,a,b,c
```

Jamie Logan

Using a function to call another function

In Python, you can call a function from within another function.
For example:

#mainbranch_sum calls the branch_sum function

```
def branch_total(m):
    return m * 2

def mainbranch_sum(n):
    return branch_total(n) + 2
```

Your output would be the following if you use the numbers 15, 7, and 12 respectively as parameter for the mainbranch)_sum:

```
>>>print(mainbranch_sum(15))        #15*2+2
32

>>>print(mainbranch_sum(7))         #7*2+2
16

>>>print(mainbranch_sum(12))        #12*2+2
26
```

Chapter 9: Classes and Object-Oriented Programming

Python is an object-oriented programming language. It means that it focuses on working with data structures collectively known as objects. An object can be anything that could be named in Python, including strings, functions, integers, classes, floats, files, and methods. Objects can refer to the data and the methods that utilize these data. They can be used in many different ways. They can be passed as arguments and assigned to variables, lists, tuples, dictionaries, or sets. Practically everything is an object in Python.

A class is a data type like strings, lists, floats, integers, or dictionaries. Class belongs to a data type called 'type'. The data values that you store inside a class object are called attributes while the functions that are associated with it are called methods. A class is simply a way to create, organize, and manage objects with similar attributes and methods. When you create objects out of a class, the object is called an instance of the class.

Defining a Class

A class definition statement starts with the keyword class followed by a class identifier and a colon. By convention, names of classes start in uppercase. A docstring which provides a short description of the class usually follows the class definition line.

Here is an example of a class definition:

```
class Furniture:
    #This is an example of a class definition.
    pass
```

The following defines a class that takes an object:

```
class Members(obj)
    #I have just defined a class that takes an object.
    pass
```

When you use the keyword 'class' to create a new class, Python responds by creating a new class object with the same name as the class identifier. This new class object contains the definition of all attributes of the class. Hence, you can use it to access the attributes of the class and to instantiate new objects of the class.

To illustrate, create a new class and name it MyClass:

```
class MyClass:
    "This is an independent class."
    y = 100
    def greet(self):
        print ('Welcome, guest!')
```

To access the attributes of MyClass:

```
>>> MyClass.y
100
```

To access the function attribute of MyClass:
```
>>> MyClass.greet
<function MyClass.greet at 0x03025D20>
```

To access the docstring of MyClass:
```
>>> MyClass.__doc__
'This is an independent class.'
```

Creating Instances of the Class

The class object which is created alongside the class can be used to create instances of the class. Creating a new object is simple. You just have to assign that object to the class with a statement like:

>>>object_a = MyClass()

To access the attributes of an object, you will use the object name as prefix right before the dot and the attribute name after the dot. An object's attribute can be a method or data attribute. Methods refer to the functions of the class. To illustrate, you can use the class definition of MyClass above and create an object out of it:

obj = MyClass()

MyClass.greet, an attribute of MyClass() is a method object because if defines a function for all objects that would be created from MyClass. Hence, obj.greet is a method object.

>>> obj.greet
<bound method MyClass.greet of <__main__.MyClass object at 0x0328DB90>>

In MyClass function definition, you might have noticed that the word self was used as argument. Yet, in the above example, the method obj.greet was called without an argument. That's because when an object calls its method, the object itself becomes the first argument. By convention, the word 'self' is used to refer to the object. If there are other arguments, you can place them after 'self'.

The __init__() method

The __init__() method is a special class constructor method which is used to initialize the object it creates. Whenever you create a new instance of the class, Python calls this initialization method. The __init__ method() takes at least one argument, 'self', to identify each object.

Examples:

```
class Performers:
   def __init__(self) :
```

```
class Performers (object):
   def __init__(self, name, skills, salary) :
```

Instance Variables

Instance variables are variables that link all instantiated objects within the class. They are required when you specify several arguments besides the 'self' in the initialization method.

For example:

```
class Performers:
  "Common base for all performers."
  counter = 0
  def __init__(self, name, skills, salary):
    self.name = name
    self.skills = skills
    self.salary = salary
```

This class definition indicates that whenever an instance of the Performers class is created, each will have a copy of the variables initialized with the __init__ method.

To illustrate, you can instantiate members of the class Performers with these expressions:

```
mem_1 = Performers("Dolly", "singer", 5000.00)
mem_2 = Performers("Jayne", 'dancer', 5000.00)
mem_3 = Performers ("Lizah", 'pole dancer', 4750.00)
```

Use the print() function to see the connection between the initialized variables and the instance variables:

```
print(mem_1.name, mem_1.skills, mem_1.salary)
print(mem_2.name, mem_2.skills, mem_2.salary)
print(mem_3.name, mem_3.skills, mem_3.salary)
```

This is what you would see on your screen:

```
Dolly singer 5000.0
Jayne dancer 5000.0
Lizah pole dancer 4750.0
```

Inheritance

Inheritance is a programming structure that allows a new class to inherit the attributes of another class. Inheritance is one of Python's important features because it promotes reusability of codes and efficiency in programming. The new class is called a derived class, child class, or subclass. The class it inherits from is called a base class, parent class, or superclass.

The syntax for defining a class that would inherit the function and variables of a parent class is:

class ChildClass(ParentClass):

For example, here is a program that creates a class named Employees:

```
class Employees(object):
    "common base for all Employees"
    def __init__(self, name, position, salary):
        self.name = name
        self.position = position
        self.salary = salary

emp1 = Employees("Robert Kerr", "Supervisor", 6000.0)
emp2 = Employees("Joshua Rice", "Staff", 3000.0)
emp3 = Employees("Rezah Jones", "Manager", 8000.0)

print(emp1.name, emp1.position, emp1.salary)
print(emp2.name, emp2.position, emp2.salary)
print(emp3.name, emp3.position, emp3.salary)
```


If you run the program, the output would be:

Robert Kerr Supervisor 6000.0
Joshua Rice Staff 3000.0
Rezah Jones Manager 8000.0

Supposing you want to create a new class, Retired, which will inherit all of the attributes of the class Employees in addition to its own attribute, your class definition might look like this:

```
class Employees(object):
    "common base for all Employees"
    def __init__(self, name, position, salary):
```

```
        self.name = name
        self.position = position
        self.salary = salary

class Retired(Employees):
    "common base for Retired employees"
    def    __init__    (self,    name,    position,    salary,
retirement_year):
        Employees.__init__(self, name, position, salary)
        self.retirement_year = retirement_year


ret1 = Retired("Don Maine", "Foreman", 4500.0, 2015)
ret2 = Retired("Ashton Jack", "Plumber", 4200.0, 2014)
ret3   =   Retired("Jane   Johnson",   "Executive   Assistant",
4000.0, 2016)


print(ret1.name,          ret1.position,          ret1.salary,
ret1.retirement_year)
print(ret2.name,          ret2.position,          ret2.salary,
ret2.retirement_year)
print(ret3.name,          ret3.position,          ret3.salary,
ret3.retirement_year)
```

When you run the program, your output would be:

```
Don Maine Foreman 4500.0 2015
Ashton Jack Plumber 4200.0 2014
Jane Johnson Executive Assistant 4000.0 2016
```

Chapter 10: Importing Modules

Importing a module allows users to access the statements, objects, and definitions it contains. You can access Python's built-in files as well modules created with Python with the import keyword.

Math Module

The math module offers many useful functions. Importing it allows users to access attributes, mathematical functions, and constants such as sin(), cosine(), pi, and square root. Once you have imported the module, you can simply use the dot notation on 'math' and write the attribute or method after the dot.

To import the math module, you'll use the keyword import:

import math

If you want to import or use specific math definitions, functions, or attributes, just type it after math and the dot like :

To import specific math definitions, attributes, or functions, you will just simply type them after math and a dot. For example:

```
>>> math.sqrt(25)
5.0
```

```
>>> math.pi
3.141592653589793
```

```
>>> math.gcd(12, 8)
4
```

Displaying the Contents of a Module

To view the methods and attributes of a module after you have imported it, you can use the built-in function dir() and provide the module's name as argument.

For example, to display the contents of math module:

```
>>>import math
>>>dir(math)
['__doc__', '__loader__', '__name__', '__package__',
'__spec__', 'acos', 'acosh', 'asin', 'asinh', 'atan', 'atan2',
'atanh', 'ceil', 'copysign', 'cos', 'cosh', 'degrees', 'e', 'erf',
'erfc', 'exp', 'expm1', 'fabs', 'factorial', 'floor', 'fmod', 'frexp',
'fsum', 'gamma', 'gcd', 'hypot', 'inf', 'isclose', 'isfinite', 'isinf',
'isnan', 'ldexp', 'lgamma', 'log', 'log10', 'log1p', 'log2', 'modf',
'nan', 'pi', 'pow', 'radians', 'sin', 'sinh', 'sqrt', 'tan', 'tanh',
'trunc']
```

The Random Module

The Random module gives access to several functions which are commonly used in game development. When you want your program to produce a random number within a range, require the user to pick a random item from a list, simulate dice roll, coin flipping, card picking, and other similar games, the random module is what you will need to import.

To import the random module:

import random

Random Functions

Importing the random module will give you access to its different functions:

randint()

The randint() function generates a random integer and accepts two parameters, the lowest and the highest integer. For example, to generate an integer from 1 to 10:

```
import random
print random.randint(1, 10)
```

The output will be any of these integers: 1, 2, 3, 4, 5, 6, 7, 8, 9, 10.

choice()

The choice() function generates a random value from a sequence.

The syntax is:

random.choice()

For example:

random.choice[('blue', 'yellow', 'orange])

This random function is often used to pick a random item from a list.

```
>>>import random
>>>my_list = [2, 3, 4, 5, 6]

>>>random.choice(my_list)
```

```
>>>print(random.choice(my_list))
4
>>>print(random.choice(my_list))
2
```

shuffle()

The shuffle() function returns a list which is sorted in
    random order.

The syntax is:

random.shuffle(list)

For example:

```
>>>from random import shuffle
>>>a_list = [[x] for x in range(10)]
>>> random.shuffle(a_list)
>>> print(a_list)
[[8], [0], [1], [7], [2], [3], [6], [4], [5], [9]]
```

Chapter 11: Managing Files

File is a named memory location that can be used to store data. Saving your files allows them to be accessed in the future when needed. Python handles file management through the file object.

File Operations

Python supports 4 basic file-related operations, namely:

- opening a file
- reading a file
- writing to a file
- closing a file

File Opening Modes

A Python file may be opened using different modes. It's important to familiarize yourself with them in order to ensure file safety and integrity.

Accessing a Text File

The following modes are available for accessing text files:

r   default mode: opens a file for reading

r+   opens a file for reading and writing

w   opens a file for writing: overwrites file of the same name or creates a new file

w+   opens file for reading and writing: overwrites file of the same name or creates a new file

a   append mode: adds data at the end of the file, creates new file if the named file is non-existent

a+   read and append mode: adds data at the end of the file, creates new file if the named file is non-existent

x   opens a file for exclusive creation

These modes are available for accessing files in binary format:

rb+   opens a file for reading and writing

wb+   opens a file for writing and reading: overwrites files of the same name or create a new one

ab+   opens a file for appending and reading

These are examples of file opening statements:

fileobj = open("myfile.txt")   #opens a file in default mode

fileobj = open(("myfile.txt", "w")   #opens a file in write mode

fileobj = open(("pict.bmp", "rb+")   #opens a binary file in read and write mode

Closing Files

Closing a file is an important step in Python file management and maintenance. Closing an open file frees up the resources used, prevents accidental modification or deletion of data, and instructs Python to write data to your file.

Here's the syntax for opening and closing a file:

```
fileobj = open("myfile.txt")          # open myfile.txt
fileobj.close()                       # close open file
```

Writing to a File

This section will illustrate how you can write data to a Python file.

First, to build a file, open a new file with the 'w' (write) mode and create a new file object to facilitate file access:

```
>>>fileobj = open("afile.txt","w") #opens a new file named 'afile.txt'
```

Now, use the write() method to write strings to afile.txt:

```
>>> fileobj.write("A file is used to store important
information.\n")
47
```

Notice that it returns the number of characters in the string. Likewise, the string is written with a new line \n character to tell Python to save it as a separate line.

```
>>> fileobj.write("You will use a file object to handle
Python files.\n")
51
```

```
>>> fileobj.write("You can store program information on a
file.\n")
45
```

Now that you're done writing to afile.txt, you must close the file:

```
>>> fileobj.close()
```

Reading Files

There are different ways to read a text file in Python:

- the readlines() method
- 'while' statement
- with an iterator
- 'with statement'

The readlines() method

The readlines() method is one of the easiest ways to open a file in Python. It makes use of the file object to access and read the entire file. You will then create a variable to store the read file and use print to view the file.

To illustrate, open afile.txt with:

fileobj = open('afile.txt', "r")

Now, create a variable 'lines' that will store text from the readlines() method:

>>> lines = fileobj.readlines()

To access the content of the file, enter lines on the prompt:

>>>lines
['A file is used to store important information.\n', 'You will use a file object to handle Python files.\n', 'You can store program information on a file.\n']

Line by Line Reading with the 'while' loop

A simple while loop is a more efficient way to read files on a per line basis. Here is a simple 'while loop':

```
# Open myfile.txt on read only mode:
fileobj = open('myfile.txt')
# Read the first line
line = fileobj.readline()


# continue reading each line until file is empty
while line:
    print(line)
    line = fileobj.readline()
fileobj.close()
```

Here's the output when you run the while loop:

A file is used to store important information.

You will use a file object to handle Python files.

You can store program information on a file.

Line by Line Reading with an Iterator

Using an iterator is another way to read text files on a per line basis. Here's a simple for loop that you can use to iterate through the myfile.txt:

```
fo = open('myfile.txt')
for line in iter(fo):
    print(line)
fo.close()
```

Your output will be similar to per line reading using while loop:

A file is used to store important information.

You will use a file object to handle Python files.

You can store program information on a file.

Using the 'with statement'

The 'with' structure facilitates safe file opening and allows Python to close the file automatically without using the close() method. You can also use it to read through each line of a file.

Here's a 'with block' that can be used to read each line on myfile.txt:

```
line_count = 0
with open('myfile.txt', 'r') as newfile:
    for line in newfile:
        line_count += 1
        print('{:>3} {}'.format(line_count, line.rstrip()))
```

When you run the code, you'll get a per line output with line numbering:

  1 A file is used to store important information.
  2 You will use a file object to handle Python files.
  3 You can store program information on a file.

Conclusion

Thank you again for downloading this book! I hope this book was able to help you be able to learn and master the many powerful features of Python as a programming language. The next step is to practice what you have learned by writing your own programs.

www.ingramcontent.com/pod-product-compliance
Lightning Source LLC
Chambersburg PA
CBHW071217050326
40689CB00011B/2347

* 9 7 8 1 5 3 7 6 2 0 8 1 7 *